REAL LIVES

Learning Resource Bank
collection:

Mahatma Gandhi

MIKE WILSON

ALBSU   The Basic
Skills Unit
Registered Charity No. 1003969

When Gandhi died in 1948,
he had no job,
and he was not rich.

He was not a king,
or a prime minister.

He was just a thin old man
dressed in a cotton cloth.

He lived a simple life.
He made his own clothes.
His last meal was goat's milk
and raw vegetables.

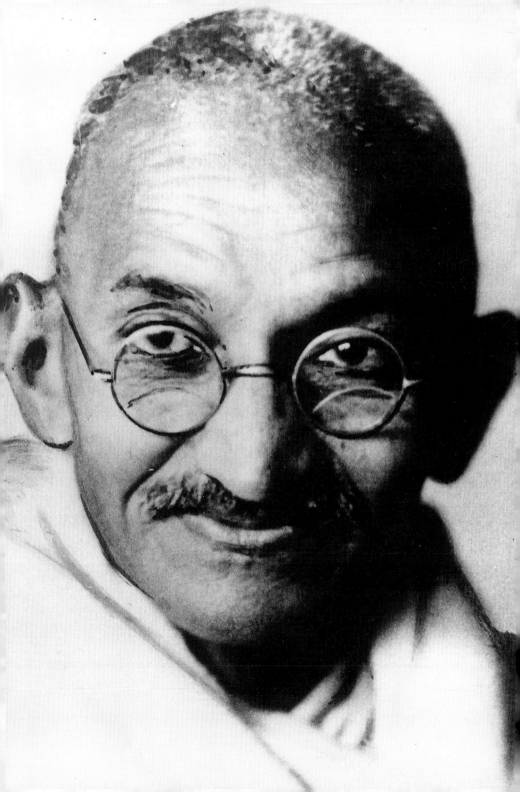

Yet one and a half million people
went to his funeral.

Famous people all over the world –
like King George the Sixth of England,
the Pope, the US President –
sent messages of sorrow.

Gandhi was famous
because he was a holy man,
a saint.

He was called a Mahatma,
which means "Great Soul".

England

Mohandas K Gandhi was born in 1869
in the Gujarat region of India.

His father and grandfather
were local officials in the Raj –
the government of the British Empire
in India.

To follow the family
into local government,
Gandhi had to study law.

So in 1888, aged 18,
he left his wife and new-born son behind
and went to London
to become a lawyer.

Three years later, in 1891,
the day after he passed his exams,
he sailed back to India.
He didn't stay in Britain
one day longer than he had to.

South Africa

In May 1893,
Gandhi went to South Africa
to work on a law case
for an Indian business man there.

He found he could not stay in hotels,
or go first class on trains,
because of the colour of his skin.

Gandhi wanted to fight
so that Indians in South Africa
would have the same freedoms
as other South Africans.

He stayed for 20 years,
fighting for human rights.

From the start, Gandhi knew
he could not fight the police and soldiers:
there were too many,
and they were too strong.

And for Hindus (like Gandhi)
it is wrong to kill any living thing.

So his fight was always peaceful:
"I am prepared to die," he said,
"but I am not prepared to kill".

Many times he was beaten,
and put in prison,
but he never hit back at his enemies.

He faced them with dignity
and with his knowledge of the law.

When he had won some freedoms
for the Indians in South Africa,
he went back to India,
to fight for human rights there as well.

8

India

When Gandhi went back to India in 1915,
he got a hero's welcome.
People wanted him to fight for Home Rule,
to get the British out of India.

But soon he settled on a little farm,
to live the simple life of a Holy Man.
He grew his own food
and made his own cloth.

People came for miles
to hear his words of wisdom.

His message to the British Raj
was loud and clear:
"It's time you left India."

9

But to the people of India he still said:
don't hit back at your enemy.
"I want to change their minds,
not kill them."
He called for all Indians to go on strike,
but he called it a day of prayer and fasting,
so it was a day of peaceful protest.

When there was fighting
between Indians and British soldiers,
Gandhi fasted.
He ate no food for days and days,
to remind people he hated violence.
In the end,
people felt ashamed of their violence,
and the fighting stopped.

He said:
"All through history,
the way of Truth and Love
has always won in the end."

Independence

India won Independence in 1948.
The British moved out,
but fighting soon broke out
between Hindus and Muslims.

Ghandi wanted all Indians
to forget their differences,
and live in peace together.

But the country split;
most of the Hindus in India,
and most of the Muslims
in East Pakistan and West Pakistan.

Ghandi planned to go to Pakistan
to show that Hindus and Muslims
could live together, pray together
and love one another.

But this was too much for some Hindus.
They were angry, and wanted to fight.

For them it was better to kill the Holy Man,
than to see him try to make peace.

On Sunday, 25th January 1948,
Nathuram Godse stood in the crowds
when Gandhi went to prayer.
He had a gun in his jacket.

He was in the front row.
When Gandhi came near,
Godse bowed to show his respect.

Then he shot the thin little man
three times in the chest
from point blank range.

Quietly, Gandhi said "Oh God",
then fell to the ground.

They took him into the house,
but he died within minutes.

In those few minutes,
the man of peace lost to the men of violence.
India lost a great leader,
and the world lost a Great Soul.